Spelling Skills

Grade 6

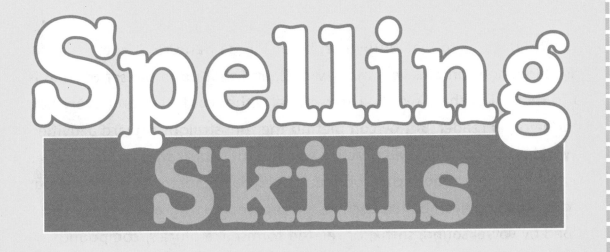

Harcourt
Family Learning™

© 2005 by Flash Kids
Adapted from *Steck-Vaughn Spelling: Linking Words to Meaning, Level 6*
by John R. Pescosolido
© 2002 by Harcourt Achieve
Licensed under special arrangement with Harcourt Achieve.

ISBN: 978-1-4114-0387-1

Please submit all inquiries to FlashKids@bn.com

Printed and bound in Canada

Lot #:
13 15 17 19 20 18 16 14
12/12

Flash Kids
A Division of Barnes & Noble
122 Fifth Avenue
New York, NY 10011

Dear Parent,

As your child learns to read and write, he or she is bound to discover that the English language contains very many words, and that no single set of rules is used to spell all of these words. This can feel rather confusing and overwhelming for a young reader. But by completing the fun, straightforward activities in this workbook, your child will practice spelling the words that he or she is most likely to encounter in both classroom and everyday reading. To make the path to proper spelling even easier, each lesson presents sixth-grade words in lists grouped by vowel sound, suffix, or related forms, like plurals, compound words, and words with suffixes. This order will clearly show your child the different ways that similar sounds can be spelled.

Each of the 30 lessons begins by asking your child to say each word in the word list. This exercise helps him or her to make the connection between a word's appearance and what it sounds like. Next, he or she will sort the words, which teaches the relationship between a sound and its spelling patterns. Your child will then encounter a variety of activities that will strengthen his or her understanding of the meaning and use of each word. These include recognizing definitions, synonyms, and parts of speech, completing analogies, as well as using capitalization and punctuation. Be sure to have a children's or adult dictionary available, which your child will need to use for some of the exercises. Each lesson also features a short passage containing spelling and grammar mistakes that your child will proofread and correct, using the proofreading marks on page 7. Once he or she can recognize both correct and incorrect spellings, your child is ready for the next lesson!

Throughout this workbook are brief unit reviews to help reinforce knowledge of the words that have been learned in the lessons. Your child can use the answer key to check his or her work in the lessons and reviews. Also, take advantage of everyday opportunities to improve spelling skills. By asking your child to read stories or newspaper articles to you at home, or billboards and signs while traveling, you are showing your child how often he or she will encounter these words. You can also give your child extra practice in writing these correct spellings by having him or her write a shopping list or note to a family member.

Since learning to spell can be frustrating, your child may wish to use one or more of the spelling strategies on page 6 when he or she finds a word or group of words difficult to master. You can also encourage your child to use the following study steps to learn a word:

1. Say the word. What consonant sounds do you hear? What vowel sounds do you hear? How many syllables do you hear?

2. Look at the letters in the word. Think about how each sound is spelled. Find any spelling patterns or parts that you know.
    Close your eyes. Picture the word in your mind.

3. Spell the word aloud.

4. Write the word. Say each letter as you write it.

5. Check the spelling. If you did not spell the word correctly, use the study steps again.

With help from you and this workbook, your child is well on the way to excellent skills in spelling, reading, and writing!

Table of contents

spelling strategies

What can you do when you aren't sure how to spell a word?

Say the word aloud. Make sure you say it correctly. Listen to the sounds in the word. Think about letters and patterns that might spell the sounds.

Look in the Spelling Table on page 141 to find common spellings for sounds in the word.

Think about related words. They may help you spell the word you're not sure of.

departure—depart

Guess the spelling of the word and check it in a dictionary.

Write the word in different ways. Compare the spellings and choose the one that looks correct.

explane explayn expleyn (explain)

Think about any spelling rules you know that can help you spell the word.

To form the plural of some singular words ending in f or fe, change f to v and add -s or -es.

knife—knives   wolf—wolves

Listen for a common word part, such as a prefix, suffix, or ending.

passage

comfortable

Break the word into syllables and think about how each syllable might be spelled.

at-mos-phere
in-cor-rect

Create a memory clue to help you remember the spelling of the word.

We told her about the weather.

6

Proofreading Marks

Mark	Meaning	Example
◯	spell correctly	I ⟨liek⟩ dogs.
⊙	add period	They are my favorite kind of pet ⊙
?	add question mark	Are you lucky enough to have a dog ?
≡	capitalize	My dog's name is s̲c̲ooter.
ℓ	take out	He is a great companion for me and my ~~my~~ family.
∧	add	We got Scooter when ∧ᵸᵉ was eight weeks old.
/	make lowercase	My U̸ncle came over to take a look at him.
∿	trade places	He watched the puppy run ⟨in around⟩ circles.
∧	add comma	"Jack ∧ that dog is a real scooter!" he told me.
⟨⟨ ⟩⟩	add quotation marks	⟨⟨Scooter! That's the perfect name! ⟩⟩ I said.
¶	indent paragraph	¶ Scooter is my best friend in the whole world. He is not only happy and loving but also the smartest dog in the world. Every morning at six o'clock, he jumps on my bed and wakes me with a bark. Then he brings me my toothbrush.

Words with /ă/

salmon	camera	magnet	graph	imagine
attract	balance	gravity	passed	sandwich
catalog	rapid	command	accent	paragraph
mammal	laughed	alphabet	scramble	photograph

Say and Listen

Say each spelling word. Listen for the /ă/ sound you hear in *salmon*.

sandwich

Think and Sort

Some of the spelling words have more than one a, but only one has the /ă/ sound. Look at the letters in each word. Think about how /ă/ is spelled. Spell each word aloud.

How many spelling patterns for /ă/ do you see?

1. Write the **nineteen** spelling words that have the *a* pattern, like *catalog*. Circle each *a* that has the /ă/ sound.

2. Write the **one** spelling word that has the *au* pattern.

1. a Words

_____   _____   _____

_____   _____   _____

_____   _____   _____

_____   _____   _____

_____   _____   _____

_____

2. au Word

_____

Clues

Write the spelling word for each clue.

1. what a tightrope walker needs _____
2. why we don't fall off the Earth _____
3. a list of available items _____
4. what a photographer uses _____
5. what iron is attracted to _____
6. what a mathematician might draw _____
7. what the Earl of Sandwich ate _____
8. a section of writing _____
9. a mark found in a dictionary _____
10. what a chinook and a sockeye are _____
11. what a bear is _____

Synonyms

Synonyms are words that have the same or almost the same meaning. Write the spelling word that is a synonym for the underlined word.

12. A parade of five hundred soldiers went by the courthouse. _____
13. The general will direct the entire army. _____
14. The flowers in my grandfather's yard draw bees. _____
15. We had to hurry to make it to the train station on time. _____
16. Victor took a snapshot of Ashley. _____
17. The speedboat raced along at a fast rate. _____
18. The audience chuckled at the comic's jokes. _____
19. Can you picture what life in space would be like? _____

Words with /ă/

salmon	camera	magnet	graph	imagine
attract	balance	gravity	passed	sandwich
catalog	rapid	command	accent	paragraph
mammal	laughed	alphabet	scramble	photograph

Proofreading

Proofread the journal entry below. Use proofreading marks to correct five spelling mistakes, three capitalization mistakes, and two unnecessary words. See the chart on page 7 to learn how to use the proofreading marks.

Proofreading Marks

◯ spell correctly
≡ capitalize
℘ take out

november 27

Today was really embarrassing. I finally received the camera that I ordered from the catilog. I wanted to try it out, so I asked Sam to go to the river with me to to fotograph fish. Sam was holding the camera when i lost my balence and fell in! He laffed and took my picture. "we have pictures of two kinds of fish," he said. "We have pictures of samin and pictures of you!" I hope he he will go with me another time. I hope I can manage to stay dry next time, too.

Language Connection

Capitalization and Punctuation

A sentence begins with a capital letter. Names of people and pets also begin with a capital letter.

A sentence ends with a period, a question mark, or an exclamation point.

> Jeffrey Watkins came to visit.
> Would Max be a good name for my new puppy?
> Rocky and Dan walked ten miles yesterday afternoon!

The sentences below contain errors in spelling, capitalization, and punctuation. Write each sentence correctly.

1. may our dog sunny march in the neihborhood parade with us

_____

_____

2. even rhonda and eric did not hesitat to jump in the river for a swim

_____

_____

3. watch out for that spider on the ranecoat next to taylor

_____

_____

4. when kelly leaves, tiger and fluffy compleyn with loud meows

_____

_____

Words with /ĕ/

length	envelope	echo	guest	treasure
tennis	pleasant	excellent	measure	metric
instead	energy	breakfast	restaurant	separate
guessed	headache	insects	against	success

Say and Listen

Say each spelling word. Listen for the /ĕ/ sound you hear in *length*.

tennis

Think and Sort

Some of the spelling words have more than one e, but only one has the /ĕ/ sound. Look at the letters in each word. Think about how /ĕ/ is spelled. Spell each word aloud.

How many spelling patterns for /ĕ/ do you see?

1. Write the **eleven** spelling words that have the *e* pattern, like *length*. Circle each *e* that has the /ĕ/ sound.

2. Write the **six** spelling words that have the *ea* pattern, like *instead*.

3. Write the **two** spelling words that have the *ue* pattern, like *guest*.

4. Write the **one** spelling word that has the *ai* pattern.

1. e Words

_____   _____   _____

_____   _____   _____

_____   _____   _____

_____   _____

2. ea Words

_____   _____   _____

_____   _____   _____

3. ue Words   **4. ai Word**

_____   _____   _____

Classifying

Write the spelling word that belongs in each group.

1. snails, worms, _____

2. volleyball, soccer, _____

3. width, height, _____

4. stomachache, earache, _____

5. company, visitor, _____

6. stamp, letter, _____

7. dinner, lunch, _____

8. great, wonderful, _____

9. riches, wealth, _____

10. supposed, suspected, _____

11. divide, set apart, _____

12. in place of, rather than, _____

Clues

Write the spelling word for each clue.

13. This is the opposite of *for*.   _____

14. This word describes a warm, calm day.   _____

15. Solar power and electricity are types of this.   _____

16. If you hear a repeated sound, it might be this. _____

17. This word names a system of measurement.   _____

18. People use rulers and yardsticks to do this.   _____

19. This is the opposite of *failure*.   _____

length	envelope	echo	guest	treasure
tennis	pleasant	excellent	measure	metric
instead	energy	breakfast	restaurant	separate
guessed	headache	insects	against	success

Proofreading

Proofread the following paragraphs from a story. Use proofreading marks to correct five spelling mistakes, two punctuation mistakes, and three missing words.

Proofreading Marks

◯ spell correctly

? add question mark

⋏ add

Marian edged along the lenth of the hallway. Where was echo

coming from Someone else in the tower behind her was shouting.

This was exellent timing. Perhaps the noise would keep any other

guests from discovering her. She needed to get into the room

with red door.

Marian leaned against the wall for a moment. Her hedache

was getting worse. She took a deep breath and tried

concentrate. This was her final chance to get the tresure

back! Would it be a sucess

The door to the room with the red door

opened. Marian gasped in surprise to

see Robin smiling down at her.

Language Connection

Punctuation

A series is a list that contains three or more single words or groups of words. A comma is used to separate the parts of a series. Notice that the final comma is placed before *and* or *or.*

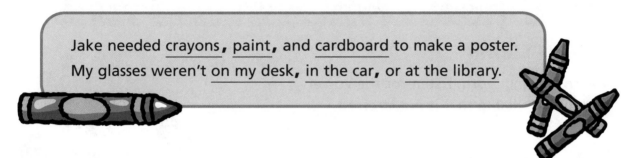

Jake needed <u>crayons</u>, <u>paint</u>, and <u>cardboard</u> to make a poster.
My glasses weren't <u>on my desk</u>, <u>in the car</u>, or <u>at the library</u>.

The following sentences contain spelling errors and errors in the use of commas. Write each sentence correctly.

1. Mother served our guest a plesant breakfast of eggs bacon, and toast.

_____

2. We all played, tennis, softball, and tag to use up our extra enegry.

_____

3. Extreme heat biting insecks, and pouring rain ruined our camping trip.

_____

4. At the restraunt we talked about hitting a home run, scoring a touchdown, and, catching a high fly.

_____

_____

5. Our guest left behind, a sealed invelope, a metric converter, and a tape measure.

_____

_____

Words with /ə/

darken	lessen	prison	lesson	captain
person	onion	strengthen	fasten	mountains
weaken	listen	lemonade	kitchen	soften
often	quicken	seldom	ransom	custom

Say and Listen

Say each spelling word. Listen for the vowel sound in the syllable that is not stressed.

Think and Sort

The weak vowel sound that you hear in unstressed syllables is called a **schwa**. It is shown as /ə/. Look at the letters in each word. Think about how /ə/ is spelled. Spell each word aloud.

How many spelling patterns for /ə/ do you see?

1. Write the **ten** spelling words that have /ə/ spelled *e*, like *fasten*.

2. Write the **eight** spelling words that have /ə/ spelled *o*, like *lesson*.

3. Write the **two** spelling words that have /ə/ spelled *ai*, like *captain*.

lemonade

---

1. e Words

_____   _____   _____

_____   _____   _____

_____   _____   _____

_____

2. o Words

_____   _____   _____

_____   _____   _____

_____   _____

3. ai Words

_____   _____

Antonyms

Write the spelling word that is an antonym of each word.

1. valleys   _____

2. harden   _____

3. lighten   _____

4. strengthen   _____

5. rarely   _____

6. frequently   _____

7. increase   _____

8. unfasten   _____

Analogies

An analogy states that two words go together in the same way as two others. Write the spelling word that completes each analogy.

9. _Eye_ is to _see_ as _ear_ is to _____.

10. _Energize_ is to _____ as _construct_ is to _build_.

11. _Sleeping_ is to _bedroom_ as _cooking_ is to _____.

12. _Kidnapper_ is to _____ as _burglar_ is to _jewelry_.

13. _Clinic_ is to _hospital_ as _jail_ is to _____.

14. _Learn_ is to _____ as _draw_ is to _picture_.

15. _Lettuce_ is to _cabbage_ as _____ is to _garlic_.

16. _Men_ is to _man_ as _people_ is to _____.

17. _Practice_ is to _____ as _rule_ is to _law_.

18. _Lemon_ is to _____ as _egg_ is to _omelet_.

19. _Length_ is to _lengthen_ as _quick_ is to _____.

Words with /ə/

darken	lessen	prison	lesson	captain
person	onion	strengthen	fasten	mountains
weaken	listen	lemonade	kitchen	soften
often	quicken	seldom	ransom	custom

Proofreading

Proofread the e-mail below. Use proofreading marks to correct five spelling mistakes, three capitalization mistakes, and two unnecessary words.

Proofreading Marks
◯ spell correctly
☰ capitalize
� take out

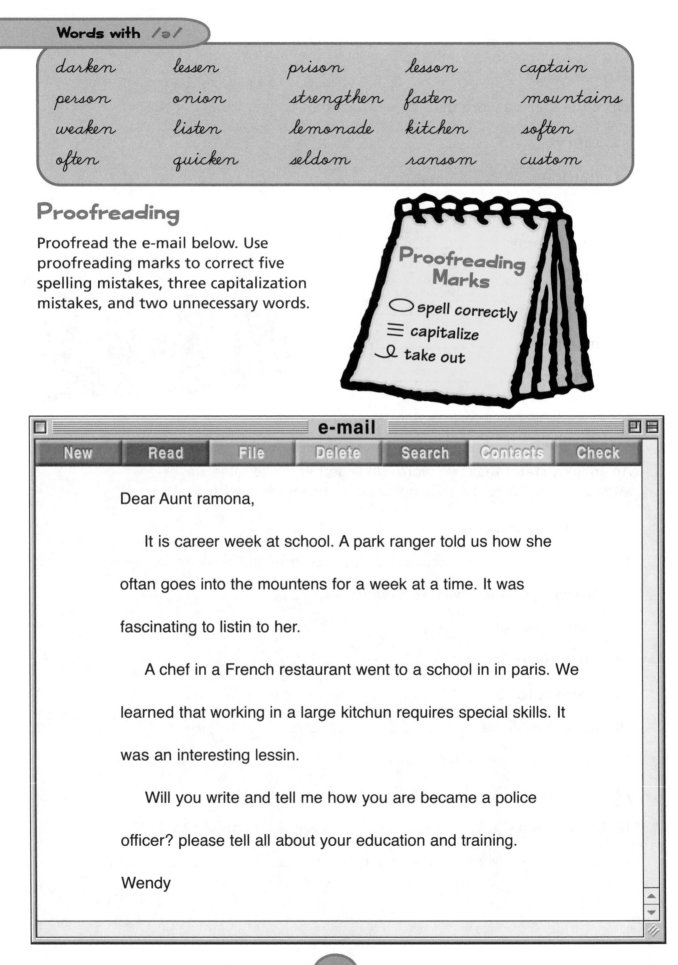

e-mail

| New | Read | File | Delete | Search | Contacts | Check |

Dear Aunt ramona,

It is career week at school. A park ranger told us how she

oftan goes into the mountens for a week at a time. It was

fascinating to listin to her.

A chef in a French restaurant went to a school in in paris. We

learned that working in a large kitchun requires special skills. It

was an interesting lessin.

Will you write and tell me how you are became a police

officer? please tell all about your education and training.

Wendy

Language Connection

Common Nouns

A common noun names any person, place, thing, or idea. A common noun is not capitalized. The common nouns in the sentence below appear in dark type.

> The **couple** arranged **flowers** in a **vase**. Their **shop** in the **market** attracted many **customers**. **Work** was an enjoyable **part** of their **life**.

Unscramble the words in the following sentences to write sensible sentences. Circle the common nouns.

1. often My television watches movies on father.

_____

2. the was about One an West old outlaw film in.

_____

3. was hiding He in a canyon mountains in the.

_____

4. seldom He had enough to eat food.

_____

5. custom It was his with open one eye to sleep.

_____

6. never found out I of the story end the.

_____

7. to the kitchen I to make went lemonade.

_____

Geography Words

Caribbean Sea	Atlantic Ocean	Africa	Andes
Himalayas	Asia	Rocky Mountains	Europe
North America	Pacific Ocean	Central America	Mississippi River
Indian Ocean	Alps	Mediterranean Sea	South America
Australia	Nile River	Appalachian Mountains	Amazon River

Say and Listen

Say the spelling words. Listen for the number of syllables in each word.

Think and Sort

All of the spelling words name places around the world. Some of the place names, such as North America, contain two words.

Rocky Mountains

1. Write the **thirteen** two-word place names, like *Caribbean Sea.*

2. A **syllable** is a word or a word part with one vowel sound. Sort the remaining **seven** spelling words by number of syllables and write them under the correct headings.

---

1. Two-word Names

_____ _____ _____

_____ _____ _____

_____ _____ _____

_____ _____ _____

_____

2. One-syllable Name   Two-syllable Names   Three-syllable Names

_____   _____   _____

                              _____   _____

Four-syllable Name   _____

_____

What's the Answer?

Write the spelling word that answers each question.

1. What mountain range is found in south-central Europe? _____

2. What is the longest river in Africa? _____

3. What body of water is found in the central United States? _____

4. What continent extends from the Atlantic Ocean to Asia? _____

Clues

Write the spelling word for each clue.

5. chief mountain range in North America _____

6. mountains in South America _____

7. highest mountains in the world _____

8. ocean between Africa and Australia _____

9. area between Mexico and South America _____

10. body of water that is part of the Atlantic Ocean _____

11. sea between Africa and Europe _____

12. largest continent _____

13. longest river in South America _____

14. continent southeast of North America _____

15. continent between Atlantic and Indian oceans _____

16. mountains found in eastern North America _____

17. continent on which Canada is located _____

18. continent between Indian and Pacific oceans _____

19. ocean just east of North America _____

Caribbean Sea	Atlantic Ocean	Africa	Andes
Himalayas	Asia	Rocky Mountains	Europe
North America	Pacific Ocean	Central America	Mississippi River
Indian Ocean	Alps	Mediterranean Sea	South America
Australia	Nile River	Appalachian Mountains	Amazon River

Proofreading

Proofread the following part of an essay. Use proofreading marks to correct five spelling mistakes, three capitalization mistakes, and two mistakes in word order.

Proofreading Marks

◯ spell correctly
≡ capitalize
∿ trade places

A Trip to Remember

by Rachel Block

First Period Language Arts

last summer my friend Akiko and her family traveled

from one coast of Narth America to the other. They

began at the New Jersey shore of the Atlantic Ocean.

Then they drove south along the Apallaichan Mountains

on their way to alabama. From they there headed

west and crossed the Missisipi River and the

Rockey Mountains. Two weeks after they started, they

ended in up Oxnard, california, at the Pacifc Ocean.

Here is the story of their trip.

Proper Nouns

Proper nouns are names of specific persons, places, or things. Each important word in a proper noun should begin with a capital letter. Notice the proper nouns in the sentences below.

> Last **August**, **Joanne** moved from **New Mexico** to **New York City**.
> She visited the **Statue of Liberty** and the **Empire State Building**.

The following sentences contain errors in capitalization. Write each sentence correctly.

1. Today my teacher, mrs. ward, talked about the climate in europe and asia.

_____

2. Then gayle pointed out the atlantic ocean, the pacific ocean, and the indian ocean.

_____

_____

3. Last month I did a report on the nile river in africa.

_____

4. I hope billy spinney will tell us about his trip to the andes.

_____

5. Last year he actually traveled down the amazon river in south america!

_____

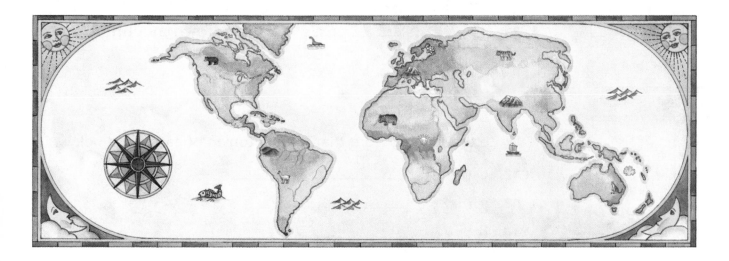

unit 1 review
Lessons 1-5

LESSON 1

accent
imagine
paragraph
salmon
laughed

Words with /ă/

Write the spelling word for each definition.

1. to form a mental picture _____

2. a manner of speech typical of a region _____

3. a fish common to northern waters _____

4. to show amusement through repeated sounds

_____

5. a part of a piece of writing _____

LESSON 2

agent
congratulate
mayor
disobey
straight
weighted

Words with /ā/

Write the spelling word that completes each sentence.

6. Did the naughty puppy _____ you?

7. Our picnic basket was _____ down with lots of food.

8. We wanted to _____ Max on his good work.

9. The sides of a square are four _____ lines of same length.

10. Our travel _____ planned a good trip for us.

11. The _____ called a town meeting yesterday.

LESSON 3

separate
measure
guessed
against

Words with /ě/

Write the spelling word that is an antonym of each word below.

12. estimate _____

13. join _____

14. for _____

15. knew _____

LESSON 4

strengthen
person
seldom
captain

Words with /ə/

Write the spelling word that belongs in each group.

16. sailor, mate, _____

17. _____, place, thing

18. toughen, improve, _____

19. rarely, _____, sometimes

LESSON 5

Central America
Pacific Ocean
Mediterranean
Sea
Mississippi
River
Appalachian
Mountains
Europe

Geography Words

Write the spelling word that identifies the place where each person is.

20. a traveler driving somewhere between Mexico and South America _____

21. a tourist visiting England, France, and Italy _____

22. a hiker on the Appalachian Trail in eastern North America _____

23. a tugboat captain along the west coast of North America _____

24. a steamboat captain docking in St. Louis, Missouri _____

25. a sailor off the coast of Greece, between Europe and Africa _____

Panama ↑

Words with /ē/

breeze	breathing	piano	piece	liter
complete	meter	memory	speaker	library
brief	ceiling	scene	repeat	extremely
degrees	gasoline	succeed	receive	increase

Say and Listen

Say each spelling word. Listen for the /ē/ sound you hear in *breeze*.

gasoline

Think and Sort

Look at the letters in each word. Think about how /ē/ is spelled.
Spell each word aloud. How many spelling patterns for /ē/ do you see?

1. Write the **five** spelling words that have the *e*, *y*, or *i* pattern, like *meter*. Circle the letter that spells /ē/ in each word.

2. Write the **eleven** spelling words that have the *ea, ee, ie,* or *ei* pattern, like *repeat*. Circle the letters that spell /ē/ in each word.

3. Write the **two** spelling words that have the *e*-consonant-*e* pattern, like *complete*.

4. Write the **one** spelling word that has both the *e*-consonant-*e* and the *y* pattern.

5. Write the **one** spelling word that has the *i*-consonant-*e* pattern.

1. e, y, i Words

_____   _____   _____

_____   _____

2. ea, ee, ie, ei Words

_____   _____   _____

_____   _____   _____

_____   _____

3. e-consonant-e Words

_____   _____

4. e-consonant-e and y Word   **5. i-consonant-e Word**

_____   _____

Classifying

Write the spelling word that belongs in each group.

1. inches, ounces, _____
2. accomplish, achieve, _____
3. add, expand, _____
4. retell, echo, _____
5. short, condensed, _____
6. thought, remembrance, _____
7. entire, whole, _____
8. accept, acquire, _____
9. very, greatly, _____
10. announcer, presenter, _____
11. eating, sleeping, _____
12. part, segment, _____
13. puff, gust, _____
14. play, act, _____
15. meter, kilogram, _____

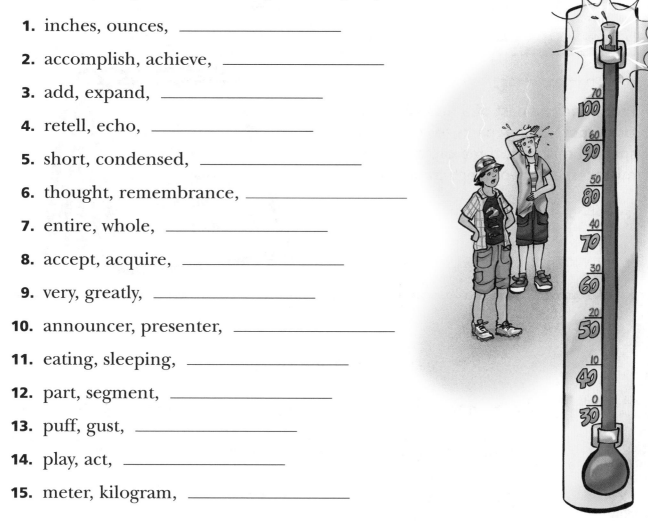

Making Connections

Complete each sentence by writing the spelling word that goes with the person.

16. A gas station attendant pumps _____.
17. A city employee reads a parking _____.
18. A pianist plays the _____.
19. A librarian helps people find books in the _____.

breeze	breathing	piano	piece	liter
complete	meter	memory	speaker	library
brief	ceiling	scene	repeat	extremely
degrees	gasoline	succeed	receive	increase

Proofreading

Proofread the part of a history report below. Use proofreading marks to correct five spelling mistakes, three capitalization mistakes, and two punctuation mistakes.

Proofreading Marks

◯ spell correctly
≡ capitalize
⊙ add period

Explorers are often the first people to travel to little-known places. many early explorers kept logs, or records, of their journeys. they knew it was extremly important to preserve the memry of each seene and event that they observed

Some explorers wrote down a compleet record of their experiences. other explorers just jotted down breif notes Their records give us important clues to life in the past. They also reveal the explorers' feelings and attitudes about the places and people they saw along the way.

Dictionary Skills

Using the Spelling Table

If you need to look up a word in a dictionary but aren't sure how to spell it, a spelling table can help. A spelling table lists common spellings for sounds. Suppose you are not sure how the vowel sound in *brief* is spelled. First, find the pronunciation symbol for the sound. Then read the first spelling listed for /ē/ and look up *bref* in a dictionary. Look for each spelling in the dictionary until you find the correct one.

Sound	Spellings	Examples
/ē/	e e_e ea ee ei eo ey i i_e ie y	meter, scene, speaker, degrees, receive, people, monkey, piano, gasoline, brief, memory

Write each of the following words, spelling the sound in dark type correctly. Use the Spelling Table on page 141 and a dictionary.

1. lăgh _____

2. trāc _____

3. gĕss _____

4. tŭch _____

5. mĭth _____

6. appēr _____

7. knŏledge _____

8. hesitāt _____

9. althō _____

10. chōs _____

Words with /ŭ/

thumb	touch	double	enough	tough
struggle	government	justice	crumb	discuss
umbrella	tongue	difficult	among	plumber
flood	trouble	compass	cousin	result

Say and Listen

Say each spelling word. Listen for the /ŭ/ sound you hear in *thumb*.

Think and Sort

Look at the letters in each word. Think about how /ŭ/ is spelled. Spell each word aloud.

How many spelling patterns for /ŭ/ do you see?

1. Write the **nine** spelling words that have the *u* pattern, like *thumb*.

2. Write the **four** spelling words that have the *o* pattern, like *among*.

3. Write the **six** spelling words that have the *ou* pattern, like *touch*.

4. Write the **one** spelling word that has the *oo* pattern.

umbrella

1. u Words

_____   _____   _____

_____   _____   _____

_____   _____   _____

2. o Words

_____   _____   _____

_____

3. ou Words

_____   _____   _____

_____   _____   _____

4. oo Word

_____

Clues

Write the spelling word for each clue.

1. This helps people to find their way. _____

2. This is very useful in rainy weather. _____

3. Congress is part of this. _____

4. This word means *sufficient*. _____

5. This word names a relative. _____

6. This word means the opposite of *easy*. _____

7. People do this when they share ideas. _____

8. This word means the same as *outcome*. _____

9. This can be the remains of a piece of toast. _____

10. People want this in a court of law. _____

11. A frog catches flies with this. _____

Rhymes

Write the spelling word that completes each sentence and rhymes with the underlined word.

12. The lights were <u>strung</u> _____ the trees in the back yard.

13. The _____ left a lot of <u>mud</u> in the cellar.

14. I'll blow a <u>bubble</u> that is _____ the size of yours!

15. It's a _____ to <u>juggle</u> four balls at once.

16. My _____ was <u>numb</u> from the cold.

17. The man's <u>gruff</u> voice makes him seem _____.

18. <u>Double</u> vision is _____ for a driver.

19. Do not _____ my <u>crutch</u> when I am walking.

Words with /ŭ/

thumb	touch	double	enough	tough
struggle	government	justice	crumb	discuss
umbrella	tongue	difficult	among	plumber
flood	trouble	compass	cousin	result

Proofreading

Proofread the letter below. Use proofreading marks to correct five spelling mistakes, three punctuation mistakes, and two unnecessary words.

Proofreading Marks

◯ spell correctly

∧ add comma

℧ take out

4100 Wilmette Lane

Chicago IL 60660

June 10 2003

Dear Captain Murphy

    My cuzin is a police officer in your squad. She said to ask you about my being a police detective. I like solving dificult problems, and I like to help people in in truble. I think I'll be good enouf for the the job when I grow up. Could you discous this with me next week? I will call you and make an appointment to see you.

        Sincerely,

        Cameron Burns

Language Connection

Subject of a Sentence

The simple subject of a sentence tells who or what is doing the action or is being talked about. It is usually one word. The complete subject of a sentence includes the simple subject and all the words that modify, or describe, it. In the example sentence below, the complete subject appears in dark type. The simple subject is underlined.

> **Several <u>members</u> of the crew** were sewing costumes for the play.

Write each of the following sentences. Circle the simple subjects and underline the complete subjects.

1. My favorite cousin lives in a small southern town.

   _____

2. A major flood badly damaged the area.

   _____

3. The federal government soon moved in to help the people.

   _____

4. The difficult struggle to survive was over.

   _____

5. My cousin's old compass was ruined in the flood.

   _____

6. His family had to hire a plumber to repair the damaged pipes.

   _____

Words with /yo͞o/ or /o͞o/

refuse	coupon	improvement	juice	humor
glue	renew	smooth	through	ruin
student	human	beautiful	threw	pollute
nuisance	canoe	rude	clue	cruel

Say and Listen

Say each spelling word. Listen for the /o͞o/ sound you hear in *refuse* and *glue*.

glue

Think and Sort

All of the spelling words have the /o͞o/ sound. In *refuse* and some other /o͞o/ words, /y/ is pronounced before the /o͞o/.

Look at the letters in each spelling word. Think about how /o͞o/ or /yo͞o/ is spelled. Spell each word aloud.

1. Write the **six** words that have the *oo* or *u* pattern, like *smooth*.
2. Write the **seven** words that have the *ew, ue,* or *u*-consonant-*e* pattern, like *threw*.
3. Write the **four** words that have the *ou, oe,* or *o*-consonant-*e* pattern, like *through*.
4. Write the **three** words that have the *ui* or *eau* pattern, like *juice*.

1. oo, u Words

_____ _____ _____
_____ _____ _____

2. ew, ue, u-consonant-e Words

_____ _____ _____
_____ _____ _____
_____

3. ou, oe, o-consonant-e Words

_____ _____ _____
_____

4. ui, eau Words

_____ _____ _____

Analogies

Write the spelling word that completes each analogy.

1. *Bicycle* is to *motorcycle* as _____ is to *motorboat*.

2. *Potato* is to *chip* as *apple* is to _____.

3. *Tremble* is to *anger* as *laugh* is to _____.

4. *Automobile* is to *car* as _____ is to *person*.

5. *Melt* is to *freeze* as *clean* is to _____.

6. *Destruction* is to *crush* as _____ is to *bother*.

7. *Unsightly* is to *ugly* as *gorgeous* is to _____.

8. *Bridge* is to *over* as *tunnel* is to _____.

9. *Improve* is to _____ as *manage* is to *management*.

10. *Discount* is to _____ as *admittance* is to *ticket*.

Synonyms

Complete each sentence with the spelling word that is a synonym of the underlined word.

11. Cold lemonade will <u>refresh</u> you and _____ your energy.

12. Marissa's skin is as _____ and <u>silky</u> as a baby's.

13. That _____ is a very strong <u>adhesive</u>.

14. Sara <u>tossed</u> the ball to Ling, who _____ it to Miguel.

15. Although he was _____ to us, we were not <u>impolite</u> to him.

16. We <u>decline</u> your offer and _____ to play.

17. His _____ actions were met with a <u>vicious</u> growl.

18. Ann's <u>hint</u> was the _____ that solved the mystery.

19. A bad fire can <u>destroy</u> property and _____ lives.

refuse	coupon	improvement	juice	humor
glue	renew	smooth	through	ruin
student	human	beautiful	threw	pollute
nuisance	canoe	rude	clue	cruel

Proofreading

Proofread the following section from a safety booklet. Use proofreading marks to correct five spelling mistakes, three capitalization mistakes, and two punctuation mistakes.

Proofreading Marks

◯ spell correctly
/ make lowercase
⊙ add period

Life Jackets may seem like a nusanse, but they are very important safety equipment. Make sure that life jackets fit the Wearers properly. A life jacket that is too big is dangerous Always remember that the belt must be securely fastened around the waist. You and your fellow boaters may not look buitiful, but you'll be safe If some of your boaters refuze to wear life jackets, do not let them remain on your Boat. You are responsible for your safety and theirs. Over time, regular use will rouin life jackets, so remember to replace them. If your life jackets are in good shape and everyone wears them properly, you'll have smyooth sailing!

Dictionary Skills

Multiple Pronunciations

Some words may be pronounced in more than one way. A dictionary gives all the acceptable pronunciations for these words, but the one listed first is generally preferred.

> **strength·en** (strĕngk′ thən) *or* (strĕng′-) *or* (strĕn′-) *v.* **strength·ened, strength·en·ing.** To make or become stronger: *Exercise helps strengthen muscles.*

Look at the pronunciations for *strengthen* given in the entry above. Notice that only the syllable that is pronounced in different ways is given in the second and third pronunciations. Study the differences in the pronunciations. Then say *strengthen* to yourself and see which pronunciation you use.

Write the spelling word for each pair of pronunciations below. Then write the pronunciation that you use. Include all of the syllables.

	Word	Pronunciation I Use
1. (stōōd′ nt) *or* (styōōd′-)	_____	_____
2. (nōō′ səns) *or* (nyōō′-)	_____	_____
3. (tə mā′ tō) *or* (-mä′-)	_____	_____
4. (kōō′ pŏn) *or* (kyōō′-)	_____	_____
5. (frăj′ əl) *or* (-īl′)	_____	_____
6. (rĭ nōō′) *or* (-nyōō′)	_____	_____
7. (rōōm′ māt′) *or* (rŏŏm′-)	_____	_____
8. (nōō′ trəl) *or* (nyōō′-)	_____	_____

Plural Words

knives	canoes	holidays	voyages	pianos
loaves	memories	industries	countries	factories
tomatoes	halves	wolves	bakeries	echoes
mysteries	mosquitoes	heroes	potatoes	libraries

Say and Listen

Say the spelling words. Listen to the ending sounds.

mosquitoes

Think and Sort

All of the spelling words are plurals. A **base word** is a word to which prefixes, suffixes, and word endings can be added to form new words. Most plurals are formed by adding -s to the base word. Other plurals are formed by adding -es. The spelling of some base words changes when -es is added.

bakery + es = baker**ies**   wolf + es = wol**ves**

Look at the letters in each word. Think about how each plural is formed. Spell each word aloud.

1. Write the **four** spelling words formed by adding -s to the base word, like *canoes.*

2. Write the **five** -es spelling words with no changes in the base word, like *echoes.*

3. Write the **eleven** -es spelling words with changes in the base word, like *wolves.*

1. -s Plurals

_____ _____ _____

_____

2. -es Plurals with No Base Word Changes

_____ _____ _____

_____ _____

3. -es Plurals with Base Word Changes

_____ _____ _____

_____ _____ _____

_____ _____ _____

_____ _____

Definitions

Write the spelling word for each definition.

1. repeated sounds bouncing off something _____

2. things that cannot be explained _____

3. people known for courage _____

4. nations or states _____

5. things that are remembered _____

6. bread baked in large pieces _____

7. groups of businesses _____

8. underground stems eaten as vegetables _____

9. two equal parts of a whole _____

Clues

Write the spelling word for each clue.

10. This vegetable is often eaten in salads. _____

11. Another word for this is *journeys*. _____

12. These are places where cars are manufactured. _____

13. Pianists play these. _____

14. These flying insects can be annoying. _____

15. People use paddles to move these. _____

16. These places sell pastries. _____

17. People borrow books at these places. _____

18. People use these to cut bread. _____

19. These animals are related to dogs. _____

knives	*canoes*	*holidays*	*voyages*	*pianos*
loaves	*memories*	*industries*	*countries*	*factories*
tomatoes	*halves*	*wolves*	*bakeries*	*echoes*
mysteries	*mosquitoes*	*heroes*	*potatoes*	*libraries*

Proofreading

Proofread the following part of a book review. Use proofreading marks to correct five spelling mistakes, three capitalization mistakes, and two unnecessary words.

Proofreading Marks

○ spell correctly

≡ capitalize

Ɑ take out

Book Review: *Everyday Heroes*

this nonfiction book deserves a shelf of its own in the libarys of countrees around the world. The people featured in the book have not sailed on dangerous voyags or or wrestled with wolffs or other wild animals. instead, they work at regular jobs in factories and bakreys. Thomas Metcalf, a steel worker from Texas, saved the lives of five people when molten steel spilled out of its vat. He is just one of the the real people in this book about unremarkable people who do remarkable things. they're all everyday heroes.

Titles of Works

Titles of long works such as books and movies appear in italic type in printed books. Because people cannot write in italics, underlining is used for these titles in handwritten materials. Quotation marks are used around the titles of short works such as poems, short stories, and songs.

> Olivia read Little Women for her last book report.
>
> Today her class read a sad poem called "Losing."

The following sentences contain misspelled words and titles that are not written correctly. Write each sentence correctly.

1. One of my heros is Julie, the main character in the book Julie of the Wolves.

2. I'm writing a poem called Holidayes of the Year.

3. I like the song Whippoorwills because of the echoze in it.

4. The movie The Red-Headed League is one of my favorite misteries.

5. My father likes the book Where the Red Fern Grows because it brings back childhood memorys.

Words with /əl/

nickel	muscle	castle	example	novel
several	vegetable	carnival	whistle	label
wrestle	hospital	bicycle	principal	tunnel
natural	grumble	general	principle	usually

Say and Listen

Say each spelling word. Listen for the /əl/ sounds you hear at the end of *nickel*.

castle

Think and Sort

Look at the letters in each word. Think about how /əl/ is spelled. Spell each word aloud.

How many spelling patterns for /əl/ do you see?

1. Write the **seven** spelling words that have the *al* pattern, like *general*.

2. Write the **four** spelling words that have the *el* pattern, like *nickel*.

3. Write the **nine** spelling words that have the *le* pattern, like *muscle*.

1. al Words

_____   _____   _____

_____   _____   _____

_____

2. el Words

_____   _____   _____

_____

3. le Words

_____   _____   _____

_____   _____   _____

_____   _____   _____

Classifying

Write the spelling word that belongs in each group.

1. circus, fair, _____

2. sample, model, _____

3. tag, sticker, _____

4. penny, _____, dime

5. complain, mutter, _____

6. lieutenant, captain, _____

7. few, some, _____

8. seldom, sometimes, _____

9. mansion, palace, _____

10. meat, grain, _____

11. student, teacher, _____

12. real, pure, _____

Making Connections

Complete each sentence by writing the spelling word that goes with the person or persons.

13. The coach showed his team the correct way to _____.

14. The famous author wrote a new _____.

15. The body builder developed his _____ tone.

16. Doctors and nurses often work in a _____.

17. The miners worked all day in the dark _____.

18. A cyclist rides a _____.

19. The referee blew her _____ at the end of the game.

nickel	muscle	castle	example	novel
several	vegetable	carnival	whistle	label
wrestle	hospital	bicycle	principal	tunnel
natural	grumble	general	principle	usually

Proofreading

Proofread the e-mail below. Use proofreading marks to correct five spelling mistakes, three capitalization mistakes, and two punctuation mistakes.

Proofreading Marks

◯ spell correctly

≡ capitalize

⊙ add period

---

e-mail

Address Book	Attachment	Check Spelling	Send	Save Draft	Cancel

Ted,

   I'm frustrated. With practice, I can usally learn to do anything, but there's one thing i can't do. It makes me grumbel to admit it, but I can't whistle It's naturel for most people, and I understand the principul behind it. Every time I try, though, only air comes out. no whistle ever comes out. I'd like to have a nickle for every time I've tried Do you have any ideas?

Later,

pete

More Words with /ə/

pencil	legend	item	balcony	cabinet
triumph	injury	amount	husband	multiply
history	atlas	balloon	focus	engine
pajamas	fortune	circus	celebrate	purpose

Say and Listen

The weak vowel sound in unstressed syllables is called **schwa** and is written as /ə/. Say each spelling word. Listen for the /ə/ sound.

balloon

Think and Sort

Look at the letters in each word. Think about how /ə/ is spelled. Spell each word aloud.

How many spelling patterns for /ə/ do you see?

1. Write the **five** spelling words that have /ə/ spelled *a*, like *balloon*.
2. Write the **three** spelling words that have /ə/ spelled *e*, like *item*.
3. Write the **four** spelling words that have /ə/ spelled *i*, like *pencil*.
4. Write the **three** spelling words that have /ə/ spelled *o*, like *history*.
5. Write the **five** spelling words that have /ə/ spelled *u*, like *circus*.

1. /ə/ Words with **a**
_____ _____ _____
_____ _____

2. /ə/ Words with **e**
_____ _____ _____

3. /ə/ Words with **i**
_____ _____ _____
_____

4. /ə/ Words with **o**
_____ _____ _____

5. /ə/ Words with **u**
_____ _____ _____
_____ _____

Kevin

marvelous
argument
departure
guitar
guard

Words with /ä/

Write the spelling word that is a synonym for the underlined word.

12. The male bird will <u>protect</u> the nest. _____

13. Gail plays the <u>lute</u> and other musical instruments.

_____

14. Tim and Fred had a <u>quarrel</u> yesterday.

_____

15. Everyone agreed that the movie was <u>wonderful</u>.

_____

16. The thief made a quick <u>exit</u> when he heard the

sirens. _____

usable
comfortable
disagreeable
terrible
possible

Words with Suffixes

Write the spelling word that completes each sentence.

17. Because I am confident, I believe it is _____
to achieve my goals.

18. My new bed is soft and _____.

19. When Lea is in a bad mood, she is very _____.

20. A broken TV is not _____ anymore.

21. Our vacation was _____ because everything
went wrong.

atmosphere
temperature
velocity
precipitation

Weather Words

Write the spelling word for each definition.

22. any form of water that falls to the ground _____

23. speed in a given direction _____

24. hotness or coldness of something _____

25. the air around the Earth _____

Clues

Write the spelling word for each clue.

1. a place to sit in a theater _____

2. what a bruise or a cut is _____

3. what people do at a birthday party _____

4. what sometimes floats high in the sky _____

5. chance or luck _____

6. what people do when they adjust a lens to get a clear image _____

7. the car part that runs _____

8. the opposite of *divide* _____

9. the story of the past _____

10. a book of maps _____

11. a synonym for *goal* _____

Classifying

Write the spelling word that belongs in each group.

12. success, victory, _____

13. myth, tale, _____

14. thing, object, _____

15. closet, cupboard, _____

16. quantity, total, _____

17. pen, marker, _____

18. carnival, fair, _____

19. father, uncle, _____

More Words with /ə/

pencil	legend	item	balcony	cabinet
triumph	injury	amount	husband	multiply
history	atlas	balloon	focus	engine
pajamas	fortune	circus	celebrate	purpose

Proofreading

Proofread the diary entry below. Use proofreading marks to correct five spelling mistakes, three capitalization mistakes, and two punctuation mistakes.

Proofreading Marks

◯ spell correctly

≡ capitalize

⊙ add period

dear Diary,

Last night a loud whooshing sound woke me I thought it was an enjen. i stepped out onto my balcany to see what it was. At first my vision was very blurry, but after I rubbed my tired eyes, I was able to focus on a huge hot-air baloon right in front of me. It had a silver top and a purple basket. A woman and her huzbind were in the balloon's basket and were waving at me. they wore a look of triumf on their faces I'm sure I wore a look of amazement on mine. It took quite a while for me to get back to sleep!

Language Connection

Apostrophes

A contraction is a shortened form of two words in which the words are joined, but one or more letters are left out. An apostrophe is used in place of the missing letter or letters.

> Do not pick the flowers.   Don't pick the flowers.
>
> They are here for display.   They're here for display.

Apostrophes are also used in the possessive form of nouns. The possessive form indicates ownership. An apostrophe and -s are added to singular nouns. Only an apostrophe is added to plural nouns that end in s. For other plurals that do not end in s, such as children, an apostrophe and -s are added.

> **Possessive Singular Noun**   **Sally's** hat is in her room.
> **Possessive Plural Noun**   The **girls'** clothes are in their closet.
> **Possessive Plural Noun**   The **mice's** home is an old tree trunk.

Write the following sentences, adding apostrophes wherever necessary.

1. Henry and his brother went to the circus to celebrate Henrys birthday.

_____

2. The boys father wanted to take them up in a hot-air balloon.

_____

3. Henry also received a set of colored pencils and a childrens atlas.

_____

4. Dads plan was for Henry to draw what he saw.

_____

Words with /ər/

cellar	modern	favorite	bother	lunar
fever	soccer	discover	similar	answer
director	vinegar	customer	governor	effort
cheeseburger	hamburger	calendar	computer	consumer

Say and Listen

Say each spelling word. Listen for the /ər/ sounds you hear in *cellar*.

computer

Think and Sort

Look at the letters in each word. Think about how /ər/ is spelled. Spell each word aloud.

How many spelling patterns for /ər/ do you see?

1. Write the **five** spelling words that have /ər/ spelled *ar*, like *cellar*.

2. Write the **eleven** spelling words that have /ər/ spelled *er*, like *answer*.

3. Write the **four** spelling words that have /ər/ spelled *or*, like *effort*.

1. /ər/ Words with **ar**

_____ _____ _____

_____ _____

2. /ər/ Words with **er**

_____ _____ _____

_____ _____ _____

_____ _____ _____

_____ _____

3. /ər/ Words with **or**

_____ _____ _____

_____

Analogies

Write the spelling word that completes each analogy.

1. *Court* is to *basketball* as *field* is to _____.

2. *State* is to _____ as *country* is to *president*.

3. *Clock* is to *day* as _____ is to *year*.

4. *Up* is to *down* as *old-fashioned* is to _____.

5. *Chills* is to *cold* as _____ is to *hot*.

6. *Movie* is to _____ as *orchestra* is to *conductor*.

7. *Attic* is to *high* as _____ is to *low*.

8. *Moon* is to _____ as *sun* is to *solar*.

9. *Push* is to *shove* as _____ is to *annoy*.

10. *Clerk* is to _____ as *waiter* is to *diner*.

Definitions

Write the spelling word for each definition. Use a dictionary if you need to.

11. a piece of cooked ground beef served on a bun   _____

12. a hamburger with cheese   _____

13. an electronic machine used at home and at work   _____

14. someone who buys and uses goods or services   _____

15. something that is liked the most   _____

16. a reply to a question   _____

17. an attempt to do something   _____

18. almost the same as   _____

19. to find out   _____

cellar modern favorite bother lunar

fever soccer discover similar answer

director vinegar customer governor effort

cheeseburger hamburger calendar computer consumer

Proofreading

Proofread the e-mail below. Use proofreading marks to correct five spelling mistakes, two punctuation mistakes, and three misplaced words.

Proofreading Marks

◯ spell correctly

⊙ add period

∿ trade places

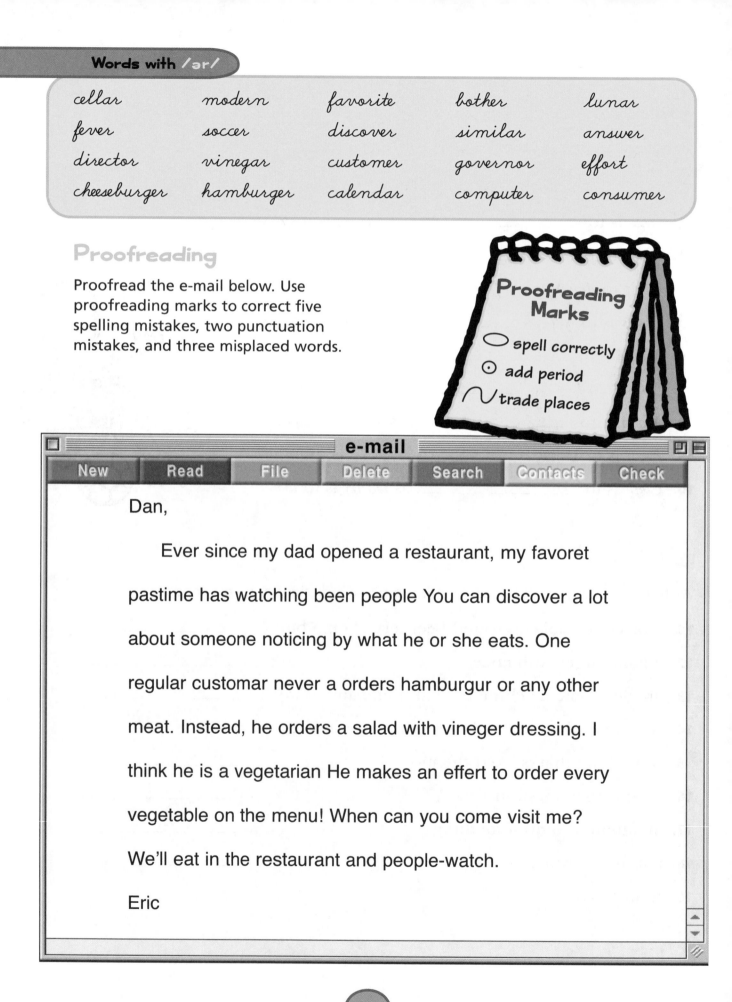

e-mail

New	Read	File	Delete	Search	Contacts	Check

Dan,

  Ever since my dad opened a restaurant, my favoret pastime has watching been people You can discover a lot about someone noticing by what he or she eats. One regular customar never a orders hamburgur or any other meat. Instead, he orders a salad with vineger dressing. I think he is a vegetarian He makes an effert to order every vegetable on the menu! When can you come visit me? We'll eat in the restaurant and people-watch.

Eric

Language Connection

Predicates

The predicate is the part of a sentence that tells what the subject of the sentence does or did, or is or was. It includes all the words that modify, or tell more about, the verb. The words of some predicates do not appear together. Study the predicates in the example sentences below.

> Today the Alleycats play a professional team.
> The game is a sellout!

Write each of the following sentences. Circle all parts of the predicate.

1. Soccer fever hit Alleyville this year.

_____

2. My sister and I rode a city bus to the stadium.

_____

3. On the way we bought a hamburger and a cheeseburger.

_____

4. With much effort the Alleycats won by three goals.

_____

5. The governor of the state congratulated the players.

_____

6. Everyone in town marked the next game on their calendar.

_____

More Words with /ə/

special	spacious	social	commercial	tremendous
courageous	generous	mysterious	various	official
jealous	delicious	efficient	nervous	dangerous
serious	genius	curious	ancient	conscious

Say and Listen

Say each spelling word. Listen for the /ə/ sound you hear in *special*.

delicious

Think and Sort

Look at the letters in each word. Think about how /ə/ is spelled. Spell each word aloud.

How many spelling patterns for /ə/ do you see?

1. Write the **thirteen** spelling words that have /ə/ spelled *ou*, like *nervous*.

2. Write the **four** spelling words that have /ə/ spelled *a*, like *special*.

3. Write the **two** spelling words that have /ə/ spelled *e*, like *ancient*.

4. Write the **one** spelling word that has /ə/ spelled *u*.

1. /ə/ Words with ou

_____   _____   _____
_____   _____   _____
_____   _____   _____
_____   _____   _____
_____

2. /ə/ Words with a

_____   _____   _____
_____

3. /ə/ Words with e

_____   _____

4. /ə/ Word with u

_____

Analogies

Write the spelling word that completes each analogy.

1. *Nature* is to *natural* as *office* is to _____.

2. *Plain* is to *homely* as _____ is to *nosy.*

3. *Thoughtful* is to _____ as *jump* is to *leap.*

4. *Skyscraper* is to *modern* as *pyramid* is to _____.

5. *Courtesy* is to *courteous* as *mystery* is to _____.

6. *Unique* is to _____ as *happy* is to *joyful.*

7. *Brilliant* is to _____ as *brave* is to *hero.*

8. *Advertisement* is to *magazine* as _____ is to *television.*

9. *Tiny* is to *petite* as _____ is to *enormous.*

10. *Unproductive* is to _____ as *empty* is to *full.*

11. *Real* is to *reality* as _____ is to *society.*

Synonyms

Complete each sentence by writing the
spelling word that is a synonym for the underlined word.

12. Our ten-room apartment is very _____. roomy

13. Fighting a forest fire is a _____ thing to do. brave

14. Sometimes Theo was a bit _____ of his best friend. envious

15. I get _____ when I have to make a speech. worried

16. The students thought of _____ ways to
solve the problem. different

17. The restaurant serves _____ food. tasty

18. Are you _____ of the fact that your shoelaces are untied? aware

19. Volunteer workers are _____ people. unselfish

special	spacious	social	commercial	tremendous
courageous	generous	mysterious	various	official
jealous	delicious	efficient	nervous	dangerous
serious	genius	curious	ancient	conscious

Proofreading

Proofread the book review below. Use proofreading marks to correct five spelling mistakes, three capitalization mistakes, and two unnecessary words.

Proofreading Marks

◯ spell correctly
≡ capitalize
ℓ take out

Book Review

The Outer Space Adventure Club is a science fiction novel full of action-packed adventures. The main character, rosa, is very nervous when she becomes an offishul member of the club. This isn't just a soshil group. The members are are serious and corajuss. they travel a tramendis number of miles to various planets and stars in our spasciuos universe. Rosa has scary experiences, but she discovers that some some very curious-looking creatures can become good friends. young adults are sure to enjoy this exciting book.

Adverbs

An adverb modifies a verb, an adjective, or another adverb by telling how, when, where, how often, or to what degree. Many adverbs end in *-ly*.

> Marco wore a brightly colored shirt.
>
> Tomorrow I will get there quickly.
>
> Deirdre skated quite beautifully.
>
> She seldom becomes angry.

Unscramble the following groups of words to write sensible sentences. Circle the adverbs.

1. woman yesterday mysterious A visited me.

_____

2. drove up a spacious car slowly in She.

_____

3. was nervous I extremely and curious.

_____

4. she was politely said official a special She that.

_____

5. questions quickly some Then she serious asked.

_____

6. send me She highly dangerous wanted to mission on a.

_____

More Words with Suffixes

attendance	sentence	constant	apparent	difference
assistant	intelligent	different	vacant	entrance
incident	performance	experience	distance	absent
assignment	instrument	ignorance	instant	distant

Say and Listen

Say each spelling word. Listen for the ending sounds.

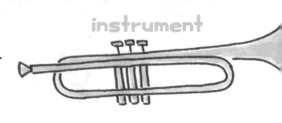

instrument

Think and Sort

Each of the spelling words in this lesson contains a suffix. A **suffix** is a word part added to the end of a base word. A suffix changes the meaning of a base word.

Look at the letters in each word. Think about how the suffix is spelled. Spell each word alo

How many suffixes do you see?

1. Write the **five** spelling words with the *-ance* suffix, like *attendance*.
2. Write the **three** spelling words with the *-ence* suffix, like *sentence*.
3. Write the **five** spelling words with the *-ant* suffix, like *instant*.
4. Write the **five** spelling words with the *-ent* suffix, like *absent*.
5. Write the **two** spelling words with the *-ment* suffix, like *instrument*.

1. -ance Words
_____ _____ _____
_____ _____

2. -ence Words
_____ _____ _____

3. -ant Words
_____ _____ _____
_____ _____

4. -ent Words
_____ _____ _____
_____ _____

5. -ment Words
_____ _____

Classifying

Write the spelling word that belongs in each group.

1. door, gate, _____

2. smart, brilliant, _____

3. helper, aide, _____

4. clear, obvious, _____

5. word, phrase, _____

6. empty, unoccupied, _____

7. event, instance, _____

8. unusual, dissimilar, _____

What's the Answer?

Write the spelling word that answers each question.

9. What does an actor in a play give? _____

10. What do you have when you have lived through an event?
_____

11. A clarinet is an example of what? _____

12. What is a lack of knowledge called? _____

13. When you aren't present, what are you? _____

14. What is the amount of space between two places? _____

15. What is a very short length of time? _____

16. The number of people who are present is called what?
_____

17. What do you call the amount of being different? _____

18. Homework is an example of what? _____

19. What word is a synonym for *continuous*? _____

attendance	sentence	constant	apparent	difference
assistant	intelligent	different	vacant	entrance
incident	performance	experience	distance	absent
assignment	instrument	ignorance	instant	distant

Proofreading

Proofread the news article below. Use proofreading marks to correct five spelling mistakes, three capitalization mistakes, and two punctuation mistakes.

Proofreading Marks

◯ spell correctly

／ make lowercase

⊙ add period

Disappointing describes last week's performance of the eagerly awaited special effects generator that has taken more than ten years to develop It soon became aparent that the new Instrument did not work. One assisstant claimed that the three-dimensional image should have appeared in an instint. The Scientists in attendance waited anxiously. Was the problem a result of the Inventor's ignorence? No one could ask its creator. The inventor was abzint from the presentation and did not return our calls

Dictionary Skills

Idioms

Sometimes a group of words does not mean exactly what it says. In the first sentence of the pair below, the tree strikes the roof when it falls. In the second sentence, however, "hit the roof" is an idiom meaning that Dad is angry; he does not actually hit the roof.

> The oak tree fell over and **hit the roof**.
> When I was late for dinner, Dad **hit the roof**.

Some dictionary entries include common idioms containing the entry word or a form of it. Study the following entry for *distance*.

> **dis·tance** (dĭs′ təns) *n.* **1.** The length of a path, especially a straight line segment, that joins two points. **2.** A stretch of space without definite limits: *a plane flying some distance off its course.* **3.** The condition of being apart in space or time.
>
> **in the distance.** In a space far removed: *Ocean Park seemed small in the distance.*
>
> **keep (one's) distance. 1.** To remain apart from; stay away from. **2.** To be aloof or unfriendly.

1. Write the two idioms given for the word *distance*.

_____

_____

Look up the following words in a dictionary. Write an idiom given for each one.

2. advantage _____

3. breath _____

4. double _____

Words with -tion or -ture

collection	attention	transportation	information	conversation
fixture	future	station	direction	invention
fraction	agriculture	election	education	lecture
correction	feature	signature	population	selection

Say and Listen

Say the spelling words. Listen for the ending sounds.

Think and Sort

Each spelling word ends in *-tion* or *-ture.* Look at the letters in each word. Think about how each word is spelled. Spell each word aloud.

1. Write the **fourteen** spelling words that have *-tion,* like *fraction.*

2. Write the **six** spelling words that have *-ture,* like *feature.*

collection

---

1. -tion Words

_____ _____ _____

_____ _____ _____

_____ _____ _____

_____ _____ _____

_____ _____

2. -ture Words

_____ _____ _____

_____ _____ _____

Word Forms

Complete each sentence by writing the spelling word that is a form of the underlined word.

1. The telephone is an exciting _____. <u>invent</u>

2. Buses are one form of _____. <u>transport</u>

3. A college _____ can be very useful. <u>educate</u>

4. Our candidate won after an exciting _____. <u>elect</u>

5. The city's _____ grew to more than a million. <u>populate</u>

6. My mother and I had a great _____. <u>converse</u>

7. I made the _____ in my report. <u>correct</u>

Definitions

Write the spelling word for each definition. Use a dictionary if you need to.

8. the act of watching and listening _____

9. things brought together for a purpose _____

10. a prepared talk given on one or more topics _____

11. a part of something that stands out _____

12. the period of time that will come _____

13. something you put in place to stay _____

14. data or facts _____

15. guidance, assistance, or supervision _____

16. the business of farming _____

17. a person's handwritten name _____

18. a regular stopping place _____

19. a choice _____

collection	attention	station	information	conversation
fixture	future	transportation	direction	invention
fraction	agriculture	election	education	lecture
correction	feature	signature	population	selection

Proofreading

Proofread the diary entry below. Use proofreading marks to correct five spelling mistakes, three capitalization mistakes, and two punctuation mistakes.

Proofreading Marks

○ spell correctly

≡ capitalize

⊙ add period

Dear Diary,

If i had a convasashun with sojourner Truth, I would give her infamasion about the dyrekshun that women's rights have taken in the past hundred years She would probably be thrilled that women now vote in each elekshun. she always hoped that women of the futer would be able to vote Would she be surprised that many women are judges, mayors, and presidents of big companies? I wonder what she would say if I told her women now run for senator, governor, and even president of the United States of America!

Dictionary Skills

Using the Spelling Table

A spelling table can help you find the spelling of a word in a dictionary. Suppose you are not sure how the vowel sound in *brief* is spelled. You can use a spelling table to find the different spellings for the sound. First, find the pronunciation symbol for the sound. Then read the first spelling listed for /ē/ and look up *bref* in a dictionary. Look for each spelling in the dictionary until you find the correct one.

Sound	Spellings	Example
/ē/	e e_e ea ee ei eo ey i i_e ie y	meter, scene, speaker, degrees, receive, people, monkey, piano, gasoline, brief, memory

Write each of the following words, spelling the sound in dark type correctly. Use the Spelling Table on page 141 and a dictionary.

1. māor _____

2. plĕsant _____

3. agĕnst _____

4. lōves _____

5. carnivəl _____

6. sĭstem _____

7. privĭt _____

8. sī _____

9. burō _____

10. lôndry _____

11. thûrsty _____

12. invisəble _____

13. balcəny _____

14. differənt _____

15. lectəre _____

16. correcshən _____

Lesson 26

balloon
celebrate
pencil
purpose
injury

More Words with /ə/

Write the spelling word that completes each sentence.

1. I like to sketch with a colored pen and _____

2. My arm hurt, but the _____ was just a sprain.

3. The red _____ popped loudly!

4. Every year we _____ the holidays with my aunt.

5. My _____ for studying is to raise my grades.

Lesson 27

calendar
answer
favorite

Words with /ər/

Write the spelling word that answers each question.

6. What do people expect when they ask a question? _____

7. What word names something you like best? _____

8. What helps people keep track of the date? _____

Lesson 28

special
ancient
efficient
conscious
mysterious
courageous

More Words with /ə/

Write the spelling word for each clue.

9. This word describes very old ruins. _____

10. If something is unusual, it is this. _____

11. This word is an antonym of *cowardly*. _____

12. This word describes something that is unknown.

_____

13. This word means "aware and awake." _____

14. This is what you are when you work without wasting time.

_____

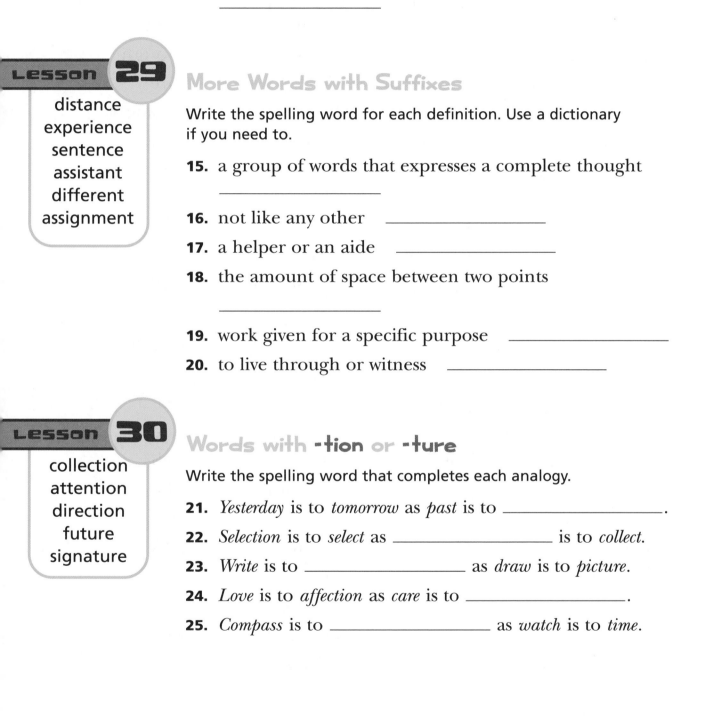

LESSON 29

distance
experience
sentence
assistant
different
assignment

More Words with Suffixes

Write the spelling word for each definition. Use a dictionary if you need to.

15. a group of words that expresses a complete thought

_____

16. not like any other _____

17. a helper or an aide _____

18. the amount of space between two points

_____

19. work given for a specific purpose _____

20. to live through or witness _____

LESSON 30

collection
attention
direction
future
signature

Words with -tion or -ture

Write the spelling word that completes each analogy.

21. _Yesterday_ is to _tomorrow_ as _past_ is to _____.

22. _Selection_ is to _select_ as _____ is to _collect_.

23. _Write_ is to _____ as _draw_ is to _picture_.

24. _Love_ is to _affection_ as _care_ is to _____.

25. _Compass_ is to _____ as _watch_ is to _time_.

commonly misspelled words

address	enough	many	they're
again	environment	might	though
a lot	especially	morning	threw
always	every	myself	through
another	everyone	once	today
anything	except	other	together
anyway	exciting	outside	tomorrow
around	family	people	too
beautiful	favorite	piece	tried
because	finally	probably	until
before	first	really	usually
beginning	friend	right	vacation
believe	friends	said	want
birthday	getting	scared	weird
bought	goes	school	were
business	guess	sent	we're
buy	happened	should	when
children	heard	since	where
clothes	himself	some	which
college	hospital	sometimes	whole
cousin	house	started	would
decided	into	surprise	write
different	it's	their	writing
doesn't	know	there	wrote
eighth	little	they	you're

spelling table

Sound	Spellings	Examples
/ă/	a ai au	catalog, plaid, laughed
/ā/	a a_e ai aigh ay ea eigh ey	agent, invade, stain, straight, mayor, break, weighted, surveyor
/ä/	a ea ua	salami, heart, guard
/âr/	are air ere eir	aware, dairy, there, their
/b/	b bb	barber, cabbage
/ch/	ch tch t	sandwich, kitchen, amateur
/d/	d dd	dawn, meddle
/ě/	e ea a ai ay ie ue	length, instead, many, against, says, friend, guest
/ē/	e e_e ea ee ei eo ey i i_e ie y	meter, scene, speaker, degrees, receive, people, monkey, piano, gasoline, brief, memory
/f/	f ff gh ph	fever, different, laugh, graph
/g/	g gg	glue, struggle
/h/	h wh	half, whole
/ĭ/	a a_e e ee ei i u ui y	spinach, luggage, select, been, forfeit, million, business, build, myth
/ī/	i i_e ie igh uy y y_e eye	science, strike, die, sigh, buy, deny, style, eye
/îr/	er ear eer eir ere yr	periodical, hear, cheer, weird, here, lyrics
/j/	j g dg	justice, voyages, pledge
/k/	k c cc ck ch	kitchen, cabinet, soccer, clockwise, choir
/ks/	x	excavation
/kw/	qu	quiet
/l/	l ll	label, umbrella
/m/	m mb mm mn	meter, thumb, mammal, condemn
/n/	n kn nn	novel, knife, tunnel
/ng/	n ng	thank, strengthen
/ŏ/	o ow a	ecology, knowledge, equality

Sound	Spellings	Examples
/ō/	o o_e oa oe ou ough ow eau ew	noble, throne, loan, toe, poultry, although, grown, plateau, sew
/oi/	oi oy	coin, enjoyable
/ô/	a au augh aw o oa ou ough	chalk, laundry, daughter, awful, often, coarse, course, thought
/ŏŏ/	oo o ou u	book, wolf, could, education
/ōō/	oo eu ew u u_e ue o o_e oe ou ui	smooth, neutral, threw, truth, refuse, clue, whom, improve, canoe, coupon, juice
/ou/	ou ow	couch, howl
/p/	p pp	pass, apply
/r/	r rh rr wr	ring, rhythm, worry, wrong
/s/	s sc ss c	slant, scene, dress, justice
/sh/	sh s ce ci	flashlight, sugar, ocean, special
/shən/	tion	station
/t/	t tt ed	tennis, attention, thanked
/th/	th	whether
/th/	th	throw
/ŭ/	u o oe oo ou	result, among, does, flood, touch
/ûr/	ear er ere ir or our ur	earn, personal, were, thirsty, worst, flourish, curly
/v/	v f	violin, of
/w/	w wh o	wind, wharf, once
/y/	y	yolk
/yōō/	eau eu u u_e	beautiful, feud, human, use
/z/	z zz s ss x	zone, quizzical, wise, dessert, xylophone
/zh/	s	treasure
/ə/	a e i o u ai ou	hospital, weaken, principle, person, circus, captain, various

Page 8
1. s@lmon, attr@ct, c@talog, m@mmal, c@mera, b@lance, r@pid, m@gnet, gr@vity, comm@nd, @lphabet, gr@ph, p@ssed, @ccent, scr@mble, im@gine, s@ndwich, p@ragraph, photogr@ph
2. laughed

Page 9
1. balance	11. mammal
2. gravity	12. passed
3. catalog	13. command
4. camera	14. attract
5. magnet	15. scramble
6. graph	16. photograph
7. sandwich	17. rapid
8. paragraph	18. laughed
9. accent	19. imagine
10. salmon	

Page 10
Spell correctly: catalog, photograph, balance, laughed, salmon
Capitalize: November, I, We
Take out: to (between "to" and "photograph"), he (between "he" and "will")

Page 11
1. accent, alphabet
2. catalog, camera
3. season, second
4. pass, people

Page 12
1. agent
2. mayor, disobey
3. tr@ce, par@de, esc@pe, inv@de, misplace, s@fety, hesit@te, congratul@te
4. complain, stain, raincoat, remain, entertain, explain
5. neighborhood, straight, weighted

Page 13
1. safety	11. escape
2. invade	12. complain
3. disobey	13. neighborhood
4. straight	14. raincoat
5. misplace	15. mayor
6. entertain	16. explain
7. remain	17. trace
8. hesitate	18. congratulate
9. weighted	19. parade
10. stain	

Page 14
Spell correctly: mayor, straight, safety, remain, entertain
Make lowercase: bands, road, parade
Add period: after "Main Street"; after "all traffic"

Page 15
1. May our dog Sunny march in the neighborhood parade with us?
2. Even Rhonda and Eric did not hesitate to jump in the river for a swim.
3. Watch out for that spider on the raincoat next to Taylor!
4. When Kelly leaves, Tiger and Fluffy complain with loud meows.

Page 16
1. l@ngth, t@nnis, @nvelope, @nergy, @cho, @xcellent, ins@cts, r@staurant, m@tric, s@parate, succ@ss
2. instead, pleasant, headache, breakfast, measure, treasure
3. guessed, guest
4. against

Page 17
1. insects	11. separate
2. tennis	12. instead
3. length	13. against
4. headache	14. pleasant
5. guest	15. energy
6. envelope	16. echo
7. breakfast	17. metric
8. excellent	18. measure
9. treasure	19. success
10. guessed	

Page 18
Spell correctly: length, excellent, headache, treasure, success
Add question mark: after "coming from"; after "a success"
Add: the (between " was" and "echo"), the (between "with" and "red"), to (between "tried" and "concentrate")

Page 19
1. Mother served our guest a pleasant breakfast of eggs, bacon, and toast.
2. We all played tennis, softball, and tag to use up our extra energy.
3. Extreme heat, biting insects, and pouring rain ruined our camping trip.
4. At the restaurant we talked about hitting a home run, scoring a touchdown, and catching a high fly.
5. Our guest left behind a sealed envelope, a metric converter, and a tape measure.

Page 20
1. darken, weaken, often, lessen, listen, quicken, strengthen, fasten, kitchen, soften
2. person, onion, prison, lemonade, seldom, lesson, ransom, custom
3. captain, mountains

Page 21
1. mountains	11. kitchen
2. soften	12. ransom
3. darken	13. prison
4. weaken	14. lesson
5. often	15. onion
6. seldom	16. person
7. lessen	17. custom
8. fasten	18. lemonade
9. listen	19. quicken
10. strengthen	

Page 22
Spell correctly: often, mountains, listen, kitchen, lesson
Capitalize: Ramona, Paris, Please
Take out: in (between "in" and "Paris"), are (between "you" and "became")

Page 23
1. My father often watches movies on television.
2. One film was about an outlaw in the old West.
3. He was hiding in a canyon in the mountains.
4. He seldom had enough food to eat.
5. It was his custom to sleep with one eye open.
6. I never found out the end of the story.
7. I went to the kitchen to make lemonade.

Page 24
1. Caribbean Sea, North America, Indian Ocean, Atlantic Ocean, Pacific Ocean, Nile River, Rocky Mountains, Central America, Mediterranean Sea, Appalachian Mountains, Mississippi River, South America, Amazon River
2. Alps
Asia, Andes, Europe
Australia, Africa
Himalayas

Page 25
1. Alps
2. Nile River
3. Mississippi River
4. Europe
5. Rocky Mountains
6. Andes
7. Himalayas
8. Indian Ocean
9. Central America
10. Caribbean Sea
11. Mediterranean Sea
12. Asia
13. Amazon River
14. South America
15. Africa
16. Appalachian Mountains
17. North America
18. Australia
19. Atlantic Ocean

Page 26
Spell correctly: North America, Appalachian Mountains, Mississippi River, Rocky Mountains, Pacific Ocean
Capitalize: Last, Alabama, California
Trade places: they/there, in/up

Page 27
1. Today my teacher, Mrs. Ward, talked about the climate in Europe and Asia.
2. Then Gayle pointed out the Atlantic Ocean, the Pacific Ocean, and the Indian Ocean.
3. Last month I did a report on the Nile River in Africa.
4. I hope Billy Spinney will tell us about his trip to the Andes.
5. Last year he actually traveled down the Amazon River in South America!

Page 28–29
1. imagine
2. accent
3. salmon
4. laughed
5. paragraph
6. disobey
7. weighted
8. congratulate
9. straight
10. agent
11. mayor
12. measure
13. separate
14. against
15. guessed
16. captain
17. person
18. strengthen
19. seldom
20. Central America
21. Europe
22. Appalachian Mountains
23. Pacific Ocean
24. Mississippi River
25. Mediterranean Sea

Page 30
1. m@ter, p@ano, memor@, l@ter, librar@
2. bre@ze, br@f, degr@es, breathing, c@ling, succ@ed, p@ce, speaker, rep@at, rec@ve, increase
3. complete, scene
4. extremely
5. gasoline

Page 31
1. degrees	11. breathing
2. succeed	12. piece
3. increase	13. breeze
4. repeat	14. scene
5. brief	15. liter
6. memory	16. gasoline
7. complete	17. meter
8. receive	18. piano
9. extremely	19. library
10. speaker	

Page 32
Spell correctly: extremely, memory, scene, complete, brief
Capitalize: Many, They, Other
Add period: after "they observed"; after "brief notes"

Page 33
1. laugh
2. trace
3. guess
4. touch
5. myth
6. appear
7. knowledge
8. hesitate
9. although
10. chose

Page 34
1. thumb, struggle, umbrella, justice, difficult, crumb, discuss, plumber, result
2. government, tongue, compass, among
3. touch, trouble, double, enough, cousin, tough
4. flood

Page 35
1. compass	11. tongue
2. umbrella	12. among
3. government	13. flood
4. enough	14. double
5. cousin	15. struggle
6. difficult	16. thumb
7. discuss	17. tough
8. result	18. trouble
9. crumb	19. touch
10. justice	

Page 36
Spell correctly: cousin, difficult, trouble, enough, discuss
Add comma: after "Chicago"; after "June 10"; after "Captain Murphy"
Take out: in (between "in" and "trouble"), the (between "the" and "job")

Page 37
1. My favorite cousin lives in a small southern town.
2. A major flood badly damaged the area.
3. The federal government soon moved in to help the people.
4. The difficult struggle to survive was over.
5. My cousin's old compass was ruined in the flood.
6. His family had to hire a plumber to repair the damaged pipes.

Page 38
1. student, human, smooth, humor, ruin, cruel
2. refuse, glue, renew, rude, threw, clue, pollute
3. coupon, canoe, improvement, through
4. nuisance, beautiful, juice

Page 39
1. canoe	11. renew
2. juice	12. smooth
3. humor	13. glue
4. human	14. threw
5. pollute	15. rude
6. nuisance	16. refuse
7. beautiful	17. cruel
8. through	18. clue
9. improvement	19. ruin
10. coupon	

Page 40
Spell correctly: nuisance, beautiful, refuse, ruin, smooth
Make lowercase: jackets, wearers, boat
Add period: after "is dangerous"; after "be safe"

Page 41
Answers for "Pronunciation I Use" will vary.
1. student
2. nuisance
3. tomato
4. coupon
5. fragile
6. renew
7. roommate
8. neutral

Page 42
1. canoes, holidays, voyages, pianos
2. tomatoes, mosquitoes, heroes, potatoes, echoes
3. knives, loaves, mysteries, memories, halves, industries, wolves, countries, bakeries, factories, libraries

Page 43
1. echoes	11. voyages
2. mysteries	12. factories
3. heroes	13. pianos
4. countries	14. mosquitoes
5. memories	15. canoes
6. loaves	16. bakeries
7. industries	17. libraries
8. potatoes	18. knives
9. halves	19. wolves
10. tomatoes	

Page 44
Spell correctly: libraries, countries, voyages, wolves, bakeries
Capitalize: This, Instead, They're
Take out: or (between "or" and wrestled"), the (between "the" and "real")

Page 45
1. One of my heroes is Julie, the main character in the book Julie of the Wolves.
2. I'm writing a poem called "Holidays of the Year."
3. I like the song "Whippoorwills" because of the echoes in it.
4. The movie The Red-Headed League is one of my favorite mysteries.
5. My father likes the book Where the Red Fern Grows because it brings back childhood memories.

Page 46
1. several, natural, hospital, carnival, general, principal, usually
2. nickel, novel, label, tunnel
3. wrestle, muscle, vegetable, grumble, castle, bicycle, example, whistle, principle

Page 47
1. carnival	11. principal
2. example	12. natural
3. label	13. wrestle
4. nickel	14. novel
5. grumble	15. muscle
6. general	16. hospital
7. several	17. tunnel
8. usually	18. bicycle
9. castle	19. whistle
10. vegetable	

Page 48
Spell correctly: usually, grumble, natural, principle, nickel
Capitalize: I, No, Pete
Add period: after "can't whistle"; after "I've tried"

Page 49
1. nickel
2. 2
3. 1

4. grumble, tunnel
5. noun, verb
6. Sentences will vary.
7. Sentences will vary.

Page 50–51
1. gasoline	14. canoe
2. piece	15. threw
3. liter	16. human
4. library	17. nuisance
5. succeed	18. coupon
6. breathing	19. cruel
7. meter	20. memories
8. receive	21. knives
9. extremely	22. pianos
10. government	23. tomatoes
11. flood	24. several
12. justice	25. principal
13. enough	

Page 52
1. million, margarine, opinion, brilliant, definite, relative, scissors, liquid
2. rhythm, myth, system
3. select, experiment
4. bus(i)n(e)ss, (e)lectr(i)c, sp(i)n(a)ch, (e)qu(i)pment, g(y)mnast(i)c, w(i)tn(e)ss, d(e)tect(i)ve

Page 53
1. scissors	11. witness
2. million	12. myth
3. liquid	13. gymnastic
4. spinach	14. detective
5. margarine	15. business
6. select	16. experiment
7. relative	17. opinion
8. brilliant	18. definite
9. rhythm	19. equipment
10. system	

Page 54
Spell correctly: brilliant, detective, opinion, business, equipment
Add period: after "a phone"; after "let me know"
Take out: to (between "to" and "start"), and (between "to" and "open"), the (between "a" and "pen")

Page 55
1. At 5:45 A.M. on April Fool's Day, my electric alarm clock rang.
2. Then I decided to conduct a brilliant experiment.
3. I switched the margarine and the butter at 6:15.
4. "This isn't margarine," my sister said at 6:45.
5. She was a good detective and no April Fool!

Page 56
1. luggage, cabbage, private, percentage, sausage, advantage, beverage, passage, message, storage, desperate, courage, average, chocolate, pirate, accurate, language, fortunate
2. (i)mmedi(a)t(e), (i)m(a)g(e)

Page 57
1. luggage	11. cabbage
2. beverage	12. image
3. fortunate	13. immediate
4. accurate	14. pirate
5. private	15. advantage
6. average	16. chocolate
7. message	17. sausage
8. language	18. desperate
9. passage	19. percentage
10. storage	

Page 58
Spell correctly: fortunate, pirate, passage, accurate, storage
Capitalize: Mexico, Friday, Pelican
Add period: after "in gold"; after "city library"

Page 59
1. choc-olate (or choco-late)
2. per-centage (or percent-age)
3. per-formances (or perform-ances)

Page 60
1. strike, surprise, survive, realize, appetite, describe, advertise, recognize
2. notify, deny, apply
3. science, violin, violet, choir, silence, design, assign
4. sigh
5. style

Page 61
1. violin	11. survive
2. appetite	12. recognize
3. science	13. apply
4. notify	14. strike
5. violet	15. describe
6. realize	16. choir
7. silence	17. style
8. design	18. sigh
9. assign	19. deny
10. surprise	

Page 62
Spell correctly: surprise, violin, describe, choir, realize
Add period: after "a solo"; after "we are"
Trade places: play/to, my/made, she/and

Page 63
1. Here (are) some suggestions that we (sent) to a TV station.
2. Always (notify) us of future programs.
3. (Realize) that we (are) intelligent viewers.
4. You (should recognize) talent at all ages.
5. (Advertise) products that (offer) us good services.
6. (Deny) time to companies that (have) false advertising.
7. (Remember) that if you (turn) us off, we (can turn) you off!

Page 64
1. merge, square
2. dis-tort, ap-pear, spi-ral, back-ground, clock-wise, re-volve, e-qual, fore-ground, pro-files, slant-ing, ob-ject
3. il-lu-sion, in-cor-rect, par-al-lel, con-cen-trate, con-stant-ly, con-tin-ue
4. un-u-su-al

Page 65
1. unusual	11. illusion
2. appear	12. parallel
3. incorrect	13. foreground
4. merge	14. revolve
5. continue	15. background
6. equal	16. profiles
7. spiral	17. object
8. constantly	18. slanting
9. clockwise	19. concentrate
10. square	

Page 66
Spell correctly: illusion, square, appear, foreground, concentrate
Add question mark: after "didn't it"; after "seeing things"
Add: to (between "had" and "be"), the (between "of" and "painting"), be (between "would" and "gone")

Page 67
1. Yes, the bright light looked unusual against the dark sky.
2. No, it didn't continue to shine past midnight.
3. Okay, it did seem to revolve around a smaller light.
4. Well, it could have been one airplane moving clockwise around another one.

Page 68
1. na-ture, wo-ven, cul-ture, frag-ile, reg-ion, cli-mate
2. in-flu-ence, re-sourc-es, be-hav-ior, skel-e-tons, ar-ti-facts, sci-en-tists, prim-i-tive, a-dapt-ed, ev-i-dence
3. so-ci-e-ty, ex-ca-va-tion, cer-e-mo-nies, i-den-ti-fy, en-vi-ron-ment

Page 69
1. artifacts	11. culture
2. nature	12. skeletons
3. resources	13. adapted
4. behavior	14. evidence
5. scientists	15. fragile
6. region	16. excavation
7. influence	17. identify
8. society	18. ceremonies
9. primitive	19. woven
10. environment	

Page 70
Spell correctly: excavation, primitive, region, skeletons, scientists
Capitalize: Last, New, These
Add period: after "Mexico"; after "shell jewelry"

Page 71
1. "I read articles about scientists digging in excavation sites," said Matthew.
2. "I have pictures of beautiful Pueblo artifacts!" exclaimed Victoria.
3. Mr. Fine said, "We are going to discuss the behavior of the Pueblo people."
4. Mr. Fine asked, "How did the environment influence their society?"

Page 72–73
1. definite	14. surprise
2. spinach	15. sigh
3. million	16. design
4. opinion	17. describe
5. electric	18. realize
6. rhythm	19. deny
7. scissors	20. science
8. message	21. parallel
9. average	22. revolve
10. desperate	23. fragile
11. private	24. environment
12. choir	25. climate
13. style	

Page 74
1. closet, ecology, comic, probably, astonish, opposite, omelet, molecule, impossible, forgotten, moccasins, proper, honor, octopus, tonsils, operate, honesty, demolish
2. equality
3. knowledge

Page 75
1. knowledge	11. ecology
2. forgotten	12. tonsils
3. honor	13. opposite
4. proper	14. comic
5. impossible	15. demolish
6. equality	16. molecule
7. omelet	17. astonish
8. closet	18. probably
9. octopus	19. operate
10. honesty	

Page 76
Spell correctly: honesty, knowledge, ecology, impossible, probably
Make lowercase: you, but, animals
Add period: after "ecology"; after "homes, too"

Page 77
1. catalog
2. omelet
3. honor
4. practise

Page 78
1. noble, poetry, solar
2. throne, telescope, propose, lone, microphone, suppose, telephone
3. loan, approach, groan
4. grown, thrown, snowy, blown
5. plateau, bureau
6. although

Page 79
1. throne	11. blown
2. loan	12. suppose
3. poetry	13. lone
4. microphone	14. noble
5. telescope	15. although
6. groan	16. thrown
7. snowy	17. grown
8. solar	18. propose
9. approach	19. plateau
10. bureau	

Page 80
Spell correctly: telescope, loan, grown, groan, propose
Add comma: after "January 25"; after "sixth graders"
Take out: it (between "it" and "around"), the (between "the" and "news"), to (between "to" and "the")

Page 81
1. /byŏor′ ō/
2. noun
3. bureaus, bureaux
4. Please telephone me tomorrow.
5. Sentences will vary.

Page 82
1. crawl, awful
2. laundry, audience, saucers, daughter, autumn, auditorium
3. sword, ordinary, support, perform, formal, chorus, forward, orchestra
4. chalk, wharf
5. course, coarse

Page 83
1. saucers	11. perform
2. wharf	12. laundry
3. coarse	13. formal
4. crawl	14. orchestra
5. sword	15. ordinary
6. chalk	16. support
7. forward	17. daughter
8. awful	18. chorus
9. autumn	19. auditorium
10. course	

Page 84
Spell correctly: perform, orchestra, auditorium, formal, audience
Capitalize: Elmer, I, March
Add comma: after "Elmer"; after "March 1"

Page 85
1. She sewed a (blue silk) gown for (her) daughter.
2. The (ancient) wharf was covered with (pink) starfish.
3. The chorus sang (our new) (school) song.
4. The (handsome) knight carried a (massive bronze) sword.
5. I put (my dirty green) shirt in the laundry.
6. (That tiny) baby will soon learn to crawl.

Page 86
1. bathrobe, passport, weekday, farewell, backpack, waterproof, proofread, chessboard, thunderstorm, flashlight, roommate, tablecloth, throughout, weekend, eavesdrop, applesauce
2. brand-new, self-confidence, old-fashioned, cross-country

Page 87
1. chessboard
2. eavesdrop
3. tablecloth
4. passport
5. backpack
6. flashlight
7. waterproof
8. cross-country
9. self-confidence
10. weekend
11. old-fashioned
12. throughout
13. proofread
14. applesauce
15. weekday
16. thunderstorm
17. roommate
18. farewell
19. bathrobe

Page 88
Spell correctly: cross-country, roommate, self-confidence, brand-new, weekend
Capitalize: Brandon, Lincoln
Take out: the (between "the" and "cross-country"), at (between "and" and "in"), an (between "have" and "my")

Page 89
1. I wore my bathrobe and slept (deeply).
2. The thunderstorm started (suddenly).
3. Our waterproof rain gear covered us (completely).
4. My flashlight shone (brightly).
5. We (hungrily) ate some applesauce.
6. (Finally) Dad and I said farewell to camping.

Page 90
1. breath, breathe, choose, chose, dairy, diary, lose, loose, quiet, quite, accept, except, desert, dessert, cloths, clothes
2. all ready, already, weather, whether

Page 91
1. clothes	11. breath
2. breathe	12. choose
3. desert	13. loose
4. dessert	14. quite
5. already	15. accept
6. quiet	16. except
7. diary	17. whether
8. weather	18. all ready
9. lose	19. chose
10. cloths	

Page 92
Spell correctly: lose, accept, choose, Whether, already
Add comma: after "selfish"; after "lazy"
Take out: in (between "are" and "told"), on (between "In" and "fables"), deeds (between "as" and "words")

Page 93
1. Either Audrey is very shy, or she is just extremely quiet.
2. Her family chose to move here, for it's a good place to start a dairy business.
3. They used to live in the desert, and it was terribly hot.
4. Audrey told us that she wore loose clothes, but she was still quite uncomfortable.

Page 94–95
1. impossible	14. chalk
2. knowledge	15. daughter
3. probably	16. awful
4. forgotten	17. coarse
5. honesty	18. course
6. equality	19. ordinary
7. opposite	20. old-fashioned
8. although	21. roommate
9. solar	22. lose
10. telephone	23. quite
11. plateau	24. quiet
12. groan	25. lose
13. thrown	

Page 96
1. blouse, doubt, couch, cloudy, mound, ouch, wound, surround, pronounce, proudly, scout, thousand
2. howl, crowded, prowl, eyebrow, allowance, coward, growled, snowplow

Page 97
1. snowplow
2. howl
3. growled
4. thousand
5. cloudy
6. crowded
7. eyebrow
8. pronounce
9. allowance
10. proudly
11. coward
12. doubt
13. Ouch
14. mound
15. scout
16. blouse
17. prowl
18. couch
19. wound

Page 98
Spell correctly: coward, doubt, prowl, howl, proudly
Capitalize: It, Wolves, The
Take out: a (between "is" and "little"), run (between "run" and "until")

Page 99
1. 2
2. 2
3. 1
4. 1

Page 100
1. refer, personal, merchant, emergency, observe, prefer, service
2. thirsty, squirrel
3. curly, purchase, furniture, disturb, current, curtains, murmur, urgent, occurred
4. worst, worry

Page 101
1. curly
2. purchase
3. urgent
4. occurred
5. disturb
6. murmur
7. worry
8. service
9. merchant
10. observe
11. refer
12. worst
13. curtains
14. thirsty
15. current
16. emergency
17. personal
18. prefer
19. furniture

Page 102
Spell correctly: purchase, observe, thirsty, furniture, disturb
Make lowercase: pet, strange, dog
Take out: the (between "new" and "pet"), to (between "to" and "purchase")

Page 103
1. adjective, noun
2. Sentences will vary.
3. Sentences will vary.
4. Sentences will vary.
5. Sentences will vary.

Page 104
1. carve, salami, barber, partner, armor, marvelous, argument, apartment, marble, marvel, scarlet, arch, harbor, regard, carpenter, guitar, departure, harmony, harmonica
2. guard

Page 105
1. arch
2. argument
3. harmonica
4. marvel
5. partner
6. marvelous
7. departure
8. regard
9. guard
10. carpenter
11. barber
12. carve
13. harmony
14. harbor
15. marble
16. apartment
17. salami
18. guitar
19. armor

Page 106
Spell correctly: marvelous, apartment, harbor, harmony, regard
Capitalize: Ginger, Here, Did
Add: the (between "near" and "harbor"), that (between "structure" and "is")

Page 107
1. guitar
2. harmonica
3. regard
4. Marvelous Music Company
5. Notes and Strings, Inc.
6. Consumer Complaint Bureau

Page 108
1. enjoyable, disagreeable, available, flammable, comfortable, breakable, usable, remarkable, valuable, reasonable, lovable, honorable, probable
2. terrible, responsible, invisible, divisible, flexible, possible, sensible

Page 109
1. breakable
2. reasonable
3. usable
4. honorable
5. sensible
6. divisible
7. enjoyable
8. responsible
9. probable
10. possible
11. lovable
12. remarkable
13. disagreeable
14. terrible
15. valuable
16. flexible
17. available
18. invisible
19. flammable

Page 110
Spell correctly: lovable, available, comfortable, responsible, valuable
Capitalize: We, Max, Can
Add period: after "a home"; after "of him"

Page 111
1. My puppy, Bongo, saved me from a (terrible) problem.
2. (Flammable) curtains were burning in the kitchen.
3. The pup knocked over a (breakable) lamp.
4. The crash of the (valuable) lamp awakened me.
5. I jumped out of my (comfortable) bed and got help.

Page 112
1. nimbus, flurries, (windchill) (forecast), (long-range), cirrus
2. atmosphere, pollution, Celsius, cumulus, Fahrenheit, prediction, (thunderhead), (overcast)
3. humidity, temperature, velocity, thermometer
4. precipitation
5. meteorologist

Page 113
1. overcast
2. forecast
3. windchill
4. long-range
5. thunderhead
6. flurries
7. Celsius
8. pollution
9. atmosphere
10. temperature
11. humidity
12. meteorologist
13. cirrus
14. Fahrenheit
15. prediction
16. precipitation
17. nimbus
18. cumulus
19. velocity

Page 114
Spell correctly: forecast, prediction, precipitation, flurries, temperature
Make lowercase: winter, snow, spring
Add comma: after "January 12"; after "freezing winds"

Page 115
1. We had some snow flurries a few weeks ago on Thanksgiving.
2. The sky was overcast, and the temperature was only 30 degrees Fahrenheit.
3. The long-range prediction is that we will have a white New Year's Day.
4. The meteorologist on TV gave the temperature tonight as 0 degrees Celsius.
5. I don't care if we have precipitation on Memorial Day, the Fourth of July, or even Labor Day.

Page 116–117
1. pronounce
2. allowance
3. crowded
4. doubt
5. proudly
6. squirrel
7. worst
8. curtains
9. furniture
10. occurred
11. emergency
12. guard
13. guitar
14. argument
15. marvelous
16. departure
17. possible
18. comfortable
19. disagreeable
20. usable
21. terrible
22. precipitation
23. velocity
24. temperature
25. atmosphere

Page 118
1. pajamas, atlas, amount, balloon, husband
2. legend, item, celebrate
3. pencil, cabinet, multiply, engine
4. history, balcony, purpose
5. triumph, injury, fortune, circus, focus

Page 119
1. balcony
2. injury
3. celebrate
4. balloon
5. fortune
6. focus
7. engine
8. multiply
9. history
10. atlas
11. purpose
12. triumph
13. legend
14. item
15. cabinet
16. amount
17. pencil
18. circus
19. husband

Page 120
Spell correctly: engine, balcony, balloon, husband, triumph
Capitalize: Dear, I, They
Add period: after "woke me"; after "their faces"

Page 121
1. Henry and his brother went to the circus to celebrate Henry's birthday.
2. The boys' father wanted to take them up in a hot-air balloon.
3. Henry also received a set of colored pencils and a children's atlas.
4. Dad's plan was for Henry to draw what he saw.

Page 122
1. cellar, vinegar, calendar, similar, lunar
2. fever, cheeseburger, modern, soccer, hamburger, discover, customer, bother, computer, answer, consumer
3. director, favorite, governor, effort

Page 123
1. soccer
2. governor
3. calendar
4. modern
5. fever
6. director
7. cellar
8. lunar
9. bother
10. customer
11. hamburger
12. cheeseburger
13. computer
14. consumer
15. favorite
16. answer
17. effort
18. similar
19. discover

Page 124
Spell correctly: favorite, customer, hamburger, vinegar, effort
Add period: after "people"; after "vegetarian"
Trade places: watching/been, noticing/by, a/orders

Page 125
1. Soccer fever (hit Alleyville) (this year.)
2. My sister and I (rode a) (city bus to the stadium.)
3. (On the way) we (bought) (a hamburger and a) (cheeseburger.)
4. (With much effort) the Alleycats (won by three goals.)
5. The governor of the state (congratulated the players.)
6. Everyone in the town (marked the next game) (on their calendar.)

Page 126
1. courageous, jealous, serious, spacious, generous, delicious, mysterious, curious, various, nervous, tremendous, dangerous, conscious
2. special, social, commercial, official
3. efficient, ancient
4. genius

Page 127
1. official
2. curious
3. serious
4. ancient
5. mysterious
6. special
7. genius
8. commercial
9. tremendous
10. efficient
11. social
12. spacious
13. courageous
14. jealous
15. nervous
16. various
17. delicious
18. conscious
19. generous

Page 128
Spell correctly: official, social, courageous, tremendous, spacious
Capitalize: Rosa, They, Young
Take out: are (between "are" and "serious"); some (between "some" and "very")

Page 129
1. A mysterious woman visited me (yesterday).
2. She drove up (slowly) in a spacious car.
3. I was (extremely) nervous and curious.
4. She (politely) said that she was a special official.
5. Then she (quickly) asked some serious questions.
6. She wanted to send me on a (highly) dangerous mission.

Page 130
1. attendance, performance, ignorance, distance, entrance
2. sentence, experience, difference
3. assistant, constant, vacant, instant, distant
4. incident, intelligent, different, apparent, absent
5. assignment, instrument

Page 131
1. entrance
2. intelligent
3. assistant
4. apparent
5. sentence
6. vacant
7. incident
8. different
9. performance
10. experience
11. instrument
12. ignorance
13. absent
14. distance
15. instant
16. attendance
17. difference
18. assignment
19. constant

Page 132
Spell correctly: apparent, assistant, instant, ignorance, absent
Make lowercase: instrument, scientists, inventor's
Add period: after "to develop"; after "our calls"

Page 133
1. in the distance; keep one's distance
2. Idiom will vary.
3. Idiom will vary.
4. Idiom will vary.

Page 134
1. collection, fraction, correction, attention, transportation, station, election, information, direction, education, population, conversation, invention, selection
2. fixture, future, agriculture, feature, signature, lecture

Page 135
1. invention
2. transportation
3. education
4. election
5. population
6. conversation
7. correction
8. attention
9. collection
10. lecture
11. feature
12. future
13. fixture
14. information
15. direction
16. agriculture
17. signature
18. station
19. selection

Page 136
Spell correctly: conversation, information, direction, election, future
Capitalize: I, Sojourner, She
Add period: after "hundred years"; after "to vote"

Page 137
1. mayor
2. pleasant
3. against
4. loaves
5. carnival
6. system
7. private
8. sigh
9. bureau
10. laundry
11. thirsty
12. invisible
13. balcony
14. different
15. lecture
16. correction

Page 138–139
1. pencil
2. injury
3. balloon
4. celebrate
5. purpose
6. answer
7. favorite
8. calendar
9. ancient
10. special
11. courageous
12. mysterious
13. conscious
14. efficient
15. sentence
16. different
17. assistant
18. distance
19. assignment
20. experience
21. future
22. collection
23. signature
24. attention
25. direction